SandCastle™

Character Concepts

Right on Time!

Kelly Doudna

Consulting Editor, Diane Craig, M.A./Reading Specialist

ABDO
Publishing Company

Published by ABDO Publishing Company, 4940 Viking Drive, Edina, Minnesota 55435.

Printed in the United States.

Credits
Edited by: Pam Price
Curriculum Coordinator: Nancy Tuminelly
Cover and Interior Design and Production: Mighty Media
Photo Credits: AbleStock, Comstock, Image 100, ShutterStock

Library of Congress Cataloging-in-Publication Data

Doudna, Kelly, 1963-
    Right on time! / Kelly Doudna.
       p. cm. -- (Character concepts)
    ISBN-13: 978-1-59928-740-9
    ISBN-10: 1-59928-740-4
    1. Punctuality--Juvenile literature. 2. School children--Conduct of life--Juvenile literature.
I. Title.

    BJ1533.P95D68 2007
    650.1'1--dc22

                                                                    2006032281

SandCastle™ books are created by a professional team of educators, reading specialists, and content developers around five essential components—phonemic awareness, phonics, vocabulary, text comprehension, and fluency—to assist young readers as they develop reading skills and strategies and increase their general knowledge. All books are written, reviewed, and leveled for guided reading, early reading intervention, and Accelerated Reader® programs for use in shared, guided, and independent reading and writing activities to support a balanced approach to literacy instruction.

Let Us Know

SandCastle would like to hear your stories about reading this book. What is your favorite page? Was there something hard that you needed help with? Share the ups and downs of learning to read. We want to hear from you! To get posted on the ABDO Publishing Company Web site, send us e-mail at:

sandcastle@abdopublishing.com

SandCastle Level: Transitional

Right on Time!

Your character is a part of who you are. It is how you act when you go somewhere. It is how you get along with other people. It is even what you do when no one is looking!

You show character by being right on time. You pay attention to what time it is. You are ready when you say you will be. You never go to school two hours late!

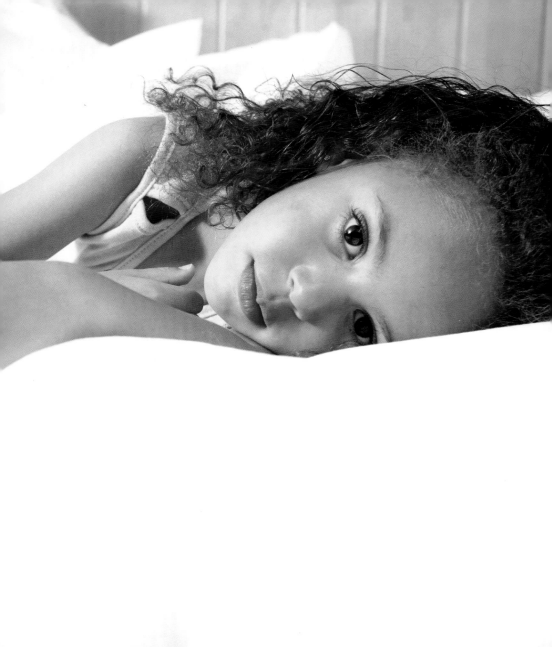

Kayla wakes up when she hears her alarm clock. She gets up and gets ready for school. Kayla is right on time.

Jordan is ready when the school bus pulls up. He doesn't make the driver wait. Jordan is right on time.

Nathan is sitting at his desk when the school bell rings. He is right on time.

Haley meets her friends at the library when she said she would. Haley is right on time.

Adam's dad picks him up after school. He waits at the meeting spot. Adam is right on time.

Right on Time!

Samantha's giant
alarm clock
sits right by her bed.
It helps her
wake up on time.
She's such a sleepyhead!

Samantha eats
her breakfast,
then grabs her
coat and bag.
She makes it to
the bus stop on time,
so no one has to nag.

18

Samantha and
her friends
plan to meet
for lunch at noon.
She gets there
right on time,
whistling a
happy tune.

Samantha heads
for home at three,
when the school
day ends.
She'll get up
on time tomorrow
and do it all again!

Did You Know?

It is hard to avoid clocks in our lives. They are everywhere, from our bedsides to our wrists to our cell phones to our microwave ovens.

Before modern clocks were invented, people used sun, sand, water, and even burning incense to tell time.

Many clocks are claimed to be the world's largest. One such clock is the Colgate Clock in Jersey City, New Jersey. It is 50 feet across.

Glossary

alarm clock – a clock that can be set to make a sound at a certain time.

nag – to constantly ask someone to do something.

sleepyhead – someone who is sleepy or is groggy from waking up.

whistle – to make a sound by blowing through puckered lips.

About SandCastle™

A professional team of educators, reading specialists, and content developers created the SandCastle™ series to support young readers as they develop reading skills and strategies and increase their general knowledge. The SandCastle™ series has four levels that correspond to early literacy development in young children. The levels are provided to help teachers and parents select appropriate books for young readers.

Emerging Readers
(no flags)

Beginning Readers
(1 flag)

Transitional Readers
(2 flags)

Fluent Readers
(3 flags)

These levels are meant only as a guide. All levels are subject to change.

To see a complete list of SandCastle™ books and other nonfiction titles from ABDO Publishing Company, visit www.abdopublishing.com or contact us at:
4940 Viking Drive, Edina, Minnesota 55435 • 1-800-800-1312 • fax: 1-952-831-1632